The Stock Market Crash of 1929: Dawn
of the Great Depression

Mary Gow

AR B.L.: 6.0

Points: 1.0   MG

The Stock Market Crash of 1929

Dawn of the Great Depression

Mary Gow

Enslow Publishers, Inc.

40 Industrial Road	PO Box 38
Box 398	Aldershot
Berkeley Heights, NJ 07922	Hants GU12 6BP
USA	UK

http://www.enslow.com

To my parents, Bob and Helen Gow

Library of Congress Cataloging-in-Publication Data

Gow, Mary.
     The stock market crash of 1929 : dawn of the Great Depression / Mary
Gow.
         v. cm. — (American disasters)
     Includes bibliographical references and index.
     Contents: Black Thursday — High-Flying decade — "A Sound Money-Making
Venture" — Crash! — Depression — Today.
     ISBN 0-7660-2111-4
     1. Stock Market Crash, 1929—Juvenile literature.
2. Depressions—1929—Juvenile literature. 3. United States—Economic
conditions—1918–1945—Juvenile literature. [1. Stock Market Crash,
1929. 2. Depressions—1929. 3. United States—Economic
conditions—1918–1945.] I. Title. II. Series.
     HB3717 1929.G68   2003
     332.64'273'09042—dc21

                                                                    2002154140

Printed in the United States of America

10 9 8 7 6 5 4 3 2 1

To Our Readers: We have done our best to make sure all Internet Addresses in this book
were active and appropriate when we went to press. However, the author and the pub-
lisher have no control over and assume no liability for the material available on those
Internet sites or on other Web sites they may link to. Any comments or suggestions can
be sent by e-mail to comments@enslow.com or to the address on the back cover.

Illustration Credits: AP/Wide World Photos, p. 7; Corel Corporation, pp. 14,
39; David Torsiello/Enslow Publishers, Inc., p. 19; Evan Zucker, p. 40; Franklin
Delano Roosevelt Library, p. 37; Hemera Technologies, Inc., 1997–2000, p. 12;
Jan Sander, p. 13; Library of Congress, pp. 10, 28, 31, 33, 35; New York in the
Thirties, As Photographed by Bernice Abbott (New York: Dover Publications,
Inc., 1967), p. 4; Steve Hewitt, pp. 17, 21; The Stock Ticker Company <www.
stocktickercompany.com>, p. 26.

Cover Illustration: Enslow Publishers, Inc.

Contents

A view of Wall Street as it appeared in the 1930s. This picture was taken from the top of the Irving Trust Company building at 1 Wall Street.

CHAPTER 1

Black Thursday

William Crawford leaned forward on the balcony above the trading floor of the New York Stock Exchange. Beneath him was a scene of confusion. More than a thousand men in suits and ties rushed about madly. They shouted and shoved. Bellowing voices, pounding footsteps, and ringing telephones joined in a roar that rumbled through the massive hall. Discarded papers covered the floor.

The New York Stock Exchange bustled on all business days. But this Thursday, October 24, 1929, was different.

Events earlier that week hinted that the stock market was headed for trouble. Thursday morning, Crawford, superintendent of the exchange, sensed "electricity in the air so thick you could cut it."[1] When the exchange opened, prices for stocks fell—fast. Panic set in. Many people wanted to sell stock. Few wanted to buy. The rules of the New York Stock Exchange stated that the stock traders were not to "run, curse, push, or go coatless."[2]

By 11:30 A.M., all those rules had been broken, forgotten in the stampede to unload stocks.

The roar in the hall was so loud that the growing crowd on Broad Street heard it. The men and women in the street were far quieter than those indoors. Some talked in hushed voices. Many stood dazed, wondering if money they had invested was gone. Extra police patrolled the street, in case the crowd got out of control. Rumors of suicides passed among the throng.

A man was spotted on a nearby roof. People watched. Was he going to jump? He did not. He was a maintenance worker making repairs.[3]

The minute hand on the exchange's clock clicked to 3:00. Crawford was ready. With a small hammer he sharply struck a brass bell.

Clang! Claang! Claaaaaang! Quivering metallic tones rang out through the hall. For an instant, the hall was silent.[4]

The brass bell had opened and closed every business day since the New York Stock Exchange moved into this building in 1903. Never before had it ended a day like this one.

October 24, 1929, is known as Black Thursday. On that day, prices of stocks in hundreds of companies collapsed. Shares of stock are small pieces of ownership in a business. When prices of stocks rise or fall by a large amount, that change has far-reaching effects. It alters the fortunes of the people who own the stocks. It affects how people feel about business and the economy. It influences the amount of money available to help businesses grow.

Edward Stone was one investor who owned many shares of stock. The Stones lived in an eleven-room apartment in a new skyscraper overlooking Central Park. Servants waited on the family.[5] Crystal, fine furniture, and hand-made rugs adorned their handsome home.

Stone's daughter, Edith, was twenty-four years old. She wore the latest styles and had her hair bobbed short. Her life was a whirl of parties. Modern young women like Edith were known as flappers.

After the stock exchange closed on Black Thursday, Edward Stone returned home. He was a changed man.

"Stop! Stop everything!" he ordered when Edith met

A large crowd gathers on the steps of the sub-treasury building across from the New York Stock Exchange on "Black Thursday," October 24, 1929.

him at the door. His eyes darted around the room. "We've got to move out!" He gazed at the furnishings, lamps, and paintings. "We can't keep any of it. I haven't a penny. The market's crashed. We're wiped out. Nothing!" Stone said. He rushed past Edith. "I'm going to kill myself. It's the only way. You'll have the insurance . . ."[6] Edith screamed for her mother. Stone pushed through the door to the terrace. The terrace was twenty stories above the street.

Edith Stone grabbed her father around the neck. Her mother tackled his knees. Stone fell to the floor. The two women saved his life.

Later, Stone explained to Edith and her mother that he had lost five million dollars in the stock market. Because of the crash, the Stones would live less lavishly.

The stock market crash of 1929 changed the lives of millions of Americans, even though only about one of every hundred Americans actually owned stock. The crash wiped out the fortunes of investors like Edward Stone. It shattered people's confidence in business. The collapse of stock prices made it difficult for many companies to raise money.[7]

After the crash, weaknesses that were already present in the U. S. economy raced out of control. Unemployment soared. Business activity declined. Factories and stores closed. Poverty and despair settled over millions of Americans. The stock market crash of 1929 marked the end of a decade of prosperity. An economic depression was already taking shape. After the stock market crash, the Great Depression engulfed the nation.

High-Flying Decade

Some called it the "Roaring Twenties." To others it was the "Jazz Age." The period from 1920 to late 1929 was a dazzling decade. Change was taking place everywhere throughout the country. American homes, transportation, communication, cities, and entertainment were transformed. The 1920s are remembered as a time of prosperity—a time when more Americans were better off than ever before.

Every year of the 1920s saw firsts. In 1920, for the first time in American history, women voted in elections. Previously, only men had the right to vote. The results of the 1920 presidential election were broadcast on the radio. It was the nation's first commercial radio broadcast. Few people heard it, though, because only about 2,000 families had radios.[1] Ten years later, radios were in twelve million homes.[2]

Some of the triumphs of the 1920s were thrilling. In 1927, Charles Lindbergh became the first man to fly solo

*M*odern young women of the 1920s were known as flappers. These two flappers dance the Charleston on a railing in Washington, D. C.

across the Atlantic Ocean to Europe. Gleaming new skyscrapers stretched taller and taller above the country's growing cities. In 1929, construction began on the Empire State Building. The 102-story marvel would be the world's tallest building for decades.

Art and entertainment were transformed in the 1920s. Jazz soared in popularity. Across the country, audiences listened to blues, ragtime, and Dixieland jazz. For the first time, many white Americans admired the talent of African-American musicians. Movies in the 1920s changed from silent films to "talkies" with music and voices. Mickey Mouse made his film debut. Radios became household fixtures. Americans sat in their homes listening to radio broadcasts of concerts, comedy shows, baseball games, and more.

Along with radios, many other changes took place in American homes. In 1920, only about one third of U. S. households had electricity. By the end of the decade, two thirds of all families had electric service. With electricity came electric lights—far cleaner than the smoky gas lamps they replaced. New electrical appliances were invented and sold. They made household jobs of cooking, cleaning, and washing easier. Families in the 1920s bought electric refrigerators to replace ice boxes. Housewives plugged in new electric irons to press clothes. Instead of beating the dirt from rugs by hand, homemakers bought vacuum cleaners to clean their carpets.

Automobiles changed American life in the 1920s more than any other new possession. With cars, Americans commuted to work. City families traveled to the country for picnics and fresh air. Country families traveled to the city for movies and concerts. Tourists drove cross-country and stayed at the new motels opening along new highways. Automobiles became the country's biggest industry. Steel, oil, tires, road building, and other automobile-related industries grew, too. Cars became families' most-prized possessions. A mother of nine children explained to a magazine reporter, "We'd rather do without clothes than give up the car."[3]

There were several reasons why so many changes came to American homes during the 1920s. Two reasons stand out: installment sales and increased efficiency of American businesses.

In the 1920s, buyers found a new way to bring more products home. Previously, most people saved their money first and bought later. Companies in the 1920s offered another choice. Instead of waiting until you had saved enough money to buy a vacuum cleaner or washing

*R*adios like this one were among the most exciting new products of the 1920s. With new technology, radios received clearer sounds than ever before.

machine, you could buy it on an installment plan. For a vacuum cleaner, you could pay $2 down and $4 every month for a year.

In the 1920s, many companies made their products faster and at lower costs than ever before. This new efficiency was key to much of the prosperity of the decade.[4]

Automobile manufacture was a spectacular example of industrial efficiency. In 1900, only 4,000 cars were made in the entire United States. They were built one at a time. A few years later, Henry Ford started making cars another way. Each worker performed a specific task. Some bolted on wheels, others attached car doors. An assembly line moved the cars to the workers. It took twelve and one-half hours to make a Model T Ford in 1912. With Ford's assembly line, it took only one and one-half hours to make the same car in 1914. In 1909, a new Model T Ford sold for $850. In 1925, a new Model T Ford cost only $290.[5]

Henry Ford sold more cars at a lower price and still made huge profits. Ford paid his workers higher wages. At the same time, he amassed a huge personal fortune.

Other companies made their factories more efficient, too. There were more cars, radios, and appliances to buy than ever before. The country had a very positive attitude about business.

"The business of America is business," said President Calvin Coolidge in 1925. "The man who builds a factory builds a temple," he said.[6] Coolidge believed American business should run without interference from the government.

"We in America today are nearer to the final triumph over poverty than ever before in the history of any land," said Herbert Hoover in 1928. Hoover was running for president of the United States. "The poorhouse is vanishing from among us," he added.[7] Hoover was elected later that year.

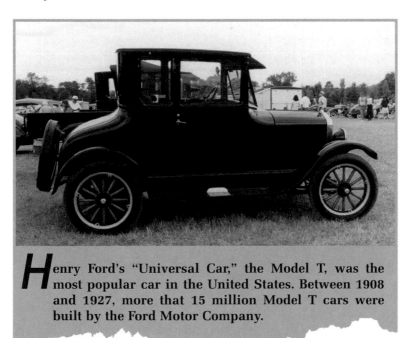

*H*enry Ford's "Universal Car," the Model T, was the most popular car in the United States. Between 1908 and 1927, more that 15 million Model T cars were built by the Ford Motor Company.

Hoover's speech reflected the optimism many people felt about the country in 1928. The United States had achieved the "highest standard of living any people had ever known."[8] All conditions, though, were not as perfect as many wanted to believe. In 1929, 42 of every 100 Americans were living in poverty. These families were trying to survive on less than $1,500 a year.[9]

Farmers did not enjoy the prosperity of the 1920s. Prices for vegetables, grain, and milk fell in the 1920s. Workers in textile mills, coal mines, and railroads missed out on the wage increases in the new efficient factories. Most African-Americans were also left out of the decade's prosperity.

There were other problems with the decade's success. Some businesses made a few people, like Henry Ford, very wealthy. Much of the country's wealth was in the hands of a small percent of the population. How the rich spent their money had a big impact on everybody else.

*A*merican cities grew and skyscrapers changed their skylines in the 1920s. In 1929, work began on the 1,250 foot-tall Empire State Building (above).

American banks were weak in the 1920s. Sometimes banks made bad decisions about how to manage money. More than 5,000 banks in the U. S. failed in the 1920s.[10] When banks failed, people lost their savings.

Overproduction was a danger in the 1920s. Companies were making more cars, radios, and appliances than ever before. The country had changed so quickly. Even with lower prices and more jobs, there was a limit to how much people would buy. In 1900, 4,000 cars were made in the U. S. In 1929, 5,358,000 cars were produced.[11] Twenty-six million cars were registered. There was one car for every five Americans. What would happen to the economy if people stopped buying cars and appliances at such a fast pace?

CHAPTER 3

"A Sound Money-Making Venture"

"**I**t was a great game," said Will Rogers, a popular entertainer and writer in the 1920s. "All you had to do was buy and wait until the next morning and just pick up the paper and see how much you made."[1] The "great game" Rogers was talking about was the stock market. For a while in the late 1920s, the stock market looked like a game that anyone could play and win.

The stock market is a general term for the business of buying and selling stocks. In the 1920s, many American companies were growing. They were building new factories, hiring more workers, and making new products. When owners of a company want to expand their business, they have several ways to raise money, such as borrowing from a bank. They sometimes sell small pieces of ownership in the business. These pieces are called shares of stock. Large companies sell millions of shares of stock.

Shares of stock are traded on stock exchanges. There

are several exchanges in the U. S. and still more in other countries. The New York Stock Exchange is the largest in the world. A stock exchange is a marketplace where stock-brokers buy and sell stocks for stock owners. The sale of stocks is a lot like an auction. Prices are determined by how much buyers will pay and sellers will accept.

How do you make or lose money on the stock market? If you buy a share of stock for $100 and the price rises to $125, you stand to make a $25 profit if you sell it. But, if the price fell to $75, you would lose $25 if you sold it.

Many factors determine how much buyers will pay for stocks. The value of a company's factories, land, and machines is something investors consider. A company's profits influence its stock price. The condition of the

Shares of stock are small pieces of ownership in companies. Stockholders receive stock certificates like the one above as proof of their ownership.

national economy is a consideration. Another important factor is whether people feel confident about business.

When stock prices are generally going up, it is called a "bull market." When stock prices are generally going down, it is called a "bear market." In 1924, stock prices began to rise. The bull market of the 1920s began.

At first, stock prices were catching up with the success of many companies. Companies sold thousands of refrigerators and washing machines. They sold millions of cars and radios. Business was good. Stock prices rose.

In 1928, the growth of the stock market changed. Instead of stock prices creeping up in little steps, they began to soar. Slow steady increases were replaced by wild leaps and bounds. Sometimes, stock prices went up several dollars in a single day. The boom took off in March.

On March 3, 1928, shares of Radio Corporation of America (RCA) stock sold for $94.50. The following Saturday, RCA shares sold for $120.50. At the end of Tuesday, March 13, RCA sold for $146.[2] In ten days, the price of RCA shares went up $51.50.

That was just the beginning. Speculation had seized the stock market. Speculation means to buy something only because you expect its price to go up.

In November 1928, Herbert Hoover was elected president of the U. S. Like President Coolidge, Hoover strongly supported business. Many speculators saw Hoover's election as another good sign for the stock market.

1928 was an incredible year for stocks. Remember the RCA stock that cost $94.50 on March 3? At the end of

December 1928, each of those shares of RCA would sell for $420.[3]

"Nothing matters as long as stocks keep going up," read a column in *The New York World* newspaper in early 1929. "The market is now its own law. The forces behind its advance are irresistible."[4] Stock prices kept bounding higher and higher.

During this stock market boom, who was buying stock? Most investors were wealthy. Some middle-class Americans with a little extra money bought stocks. These shopkeepers, secretaries, and schoolteachers purchased small amounts of stock. Stock-brokers sometimes called them minnows. Banks and investment trusts bought

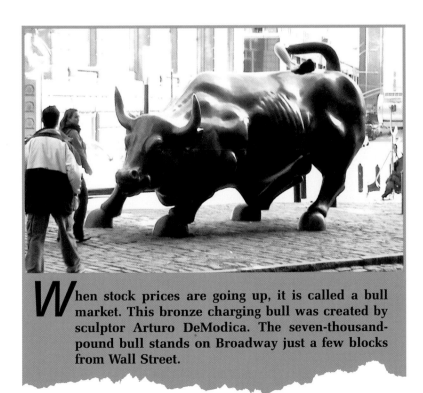

When stock prices are going up, it is called a bull market. This bronze charging bull was created by sculptor Arturo DeModica. The seven-thousand-pound bull stands on Broadway just a few blocks from Wall Street.

thousands of shares of stock. Investment trusts were companies set up for the purpose of buying and selling stocks.

Many new investors came to the stock market. Groucho Marx was one of them. Marx and three of his brothers performed comedy shows. In 1929, the Marx Brothers starred in their first movie, *The Cocoanuts.* Zany, slapstick humor was their trademark.

Groucho Marx had always been cautious with his money. But, when stock market fever swept the country, he decided to invest.

"He was in it," explained his son, Arthur, years later, "because, like everyone else he was convinced it was a sound money-making venture."[5]

The exact number of stockholders in the 1920s is not known. Investigations later indicated that perhaps one million people invested. In the 1920s, many minnows, wealthy investors, and investment trusts bought stocks with borrowed money. These loans were called buying on margin.

Margin worked like this: Suppose you wanted to buy one share of RCA when the price was $100. You only need-ed to give the stockbroker $10 instead of the full $100. The amount you paid was called the margin. The broker would loan you the difference between your payment and the full price. Suppose you sold your share when the price reached $300. You would pay the broker the $90 you owed him and a fee for loaning you the money. You would walk away with about $200. Not bad for a $10 investment!

While stock prices went up, margin loans were a terrific deal. If prices went down, however, the stockholder owed the broker money. The broker would call on the stockholder to pay the loan. This was known as a margin call.

The boom continued and prices kept soaring. Stories spread about easy fortunes. A nurse supposedly made $30,000 by investing based on stock tips from her patients. A valet who worked for a stockbroker reportedly made a quarter of a million dollars on his investments.[6] With a few shares of stock, people had dreams of vacation homes and never working again.

This promotional poster shows brothers Groucho, Harpo, and Chico Marx. Groucho Marx, in the front, was widely recognized with his bushy black eyebrows, mustache, and glasses.

Dreams were important to the way many people felt about the stock market. When stock prices went up, people felt like they had more money. Remember your $100 share of RCA stock? When its price reached $300, you might feel like you actually had $300. You might feel like you could afford to buy a nicer car or new radio. But, unless you sold the share of stock, you did not really have the money. Until you sold the stock, your gain was a "paper profit." On paper, you had more money, but you did not have more money in your pocket.

The summer of 1929 saw spectacular gains on the stock market. Some stock prices increased more than $100 per share over just three months. General Electric soared from $268 per share to $391. Telephone and Telegraph leapt from $209 to $303.

"Everybody Ought to be Rich" was the title of an article in the August 1929 edition of *Ladies Home Journal.* In it, John Jacob Raskob, a very wealthy investor, offered his advice. If a man saves $15 a month, Raskob said, "If he invests in good common stocks. . . at the end of twenty years he will have at least $80,000 and an income from investments of around $400 a month. He will be rich."[7] Average working Americans in 1929 made about $125 each month. Fifteen dollars was a lot for them to save.

Evangeline Adams was a popular New York City fortune-teller. On September 2, 1929, a radio announcer asked her prediction for the stock market. It could "climb to heaven," she replied.[8]

September 3, the day after her prediction, was blazing hot in New York City. It was also a big day for the stock market. Prices soared high—dangerously high. In fact, the prices paid for several important stocks on this day would not be seen again until November 1954.

CHAPTER 4

Crash!

"**S**ooner or later a crash is coming and it may be terrific," said Roger Babson at a business conference on September 5, 1929. "Factories will shut down . . . men will be thrown out of work."[1] Babson, a well-known economist, believed that the stock prices had been driven too high by people borrowing and speculating. Babson's remarks were published in newspapers. Many people feared that he was right. Stock prices fell the next day. A few days after Babson's comments, prices bobbed up. Most were not quite as high, though, as they had been. In October, drops in stock prices became more alarming.

On Monday morning, October 21, Groucho Marx's phone rang.

"There's been a slight break in the market, Mr. Marx," his stockbroker said. "You'd better get down here with some cash to cover your margin."

"I thought I was covered," Marx replied.

"Not enough for the way things are going. We'll need more and you'd better hurry."[2]

That morning, prices of many stocks had fallen. Groucho Marx owned stock in a company called Auburn Auto. He had bought the shares on margin. Auburn Auto's price had tumbled. Marx took money to his broker.

As prices fell, brokers telephoned and telegraphed margin calls to their clients. If the stockholders did not cover their margin, the brokers ordered the sale of the stock. On Wednesday, October 23, prices fell again.

On Thursday morning, October 24, the stock traders at the New York Stock Exchange expected a frantic day. They knew the margin on many investments had not been covered. A flood of orders waited to be sold.

At 10:00 A.M., William Crawford struck the opening bell. Stocks began selling at a furious pace. At first, there were enough buyers for sellers. Suddenly, there were more orders to sell than people willing to buy. Prices fell and panic took over. Traders shoved and shouted to get their orders sold to the few remaining investors.

Out on Broad Street a crowd began to gather. Police arrived to make sure the atmosphere stayed peaceful.

Customers packed into stockbrokers' offices. They wanted to know what was happening. How far had prices fallen? Had their brokers sold their accounts? Investors soon discovered that they could not get answers. The stock ticker was a special telegraph machine that reported stock sales as they occurred. But sales were happening too fast for the telegraph. The ticker lagged far behind the events at the exchange.

Some stockholders were angry; others were terrified. A young man recalled a woman in his broker's office. She was "wearing a big fancy hat," he said. "She's holding out her wedding ring and shouting, 'you want more margin— you can't have more margin.'"[3]

All morning at the New York Stock Exchange, panic reigned. Around noon, word reached the floor that a group of New York's most prominent bankers had met. They decided to spend several million dollars apiece to buy stocks. They hoped that when other investors saw that they were still buying, it would restore confidence in the stock market. At 1:30, Richard Whitney entered the trading hall. Representing the bankers, Whitney bought thousands of shares of stock. The purchases had exactly the effect the bankers wanted. Prices of many stocks stopped falling.

Groucho Marx borrowed money to cover his margin. But the price of his stock kept falling and even more margin was required. At the end of Black Thursday, Marx had spent all of his money and lost his stock, too. "All I lost was two hundred and forty thousand dollars," he later said. "I would have lost more but that was all the money I had."[4]

Black Thursday was bad, but worse was still to come. Stock prices flickered up a bit on Friday. They fell again on Saturday. Monday, the disaster continued.

"It was a country-wide collapse," reported *The New*

*T*he stock ticker was a special telegraph machine that printed information about stock sales. With stock tickers, investors all over the country could receive almost instant information about stock prices.

York Times about Monday's stock sales. Fewer shares of stock sold on Monday, but prices fell lower than on Black Thursday.

The New York Stock Exchange tried to prepare for Tuesday. Extra police were on the street. Doctors and nurses were on hand to provide emergency medical care. William Crawford spent Monday night repairing the exchange's stock tickers. He wanted to be sure that they would communicate sales instantly.

On Tuesday, October 29, at 10:00 A.M., Crawford rang the opening bell. An avalanche of trading began. Prices plummeted. Some stocks, like Westinghouse, lost $2 per share per minute. The Blue Ridge Investment Trust opened at $10 per share and fell to $3 in a blink. For a time, General Electric lost $1 per share every ten seconds.[5]

It was a wild scene on the trading floor. Brokers frantically scrambled to find buyers. Phones rang, messenger boys ran. One delivery service had extra supplies of smelling salts on hand to revive those who fainted.

"They roared like a lot of lions and tigers. They hollered and screamed, they clawed at one another's collars," Crawford said later. "It was like a bunch of crazy men."[6] These were the same traders who were not supposed to "run, curse, push, or go coatless."

In the madness, one broker fell to the floor. He thrashed about on the ground. A nurse came to help him. She could not understand his sputtering. A doctor arrived. He examined the fallen trader and realized that the man's false teeth were missing. His dentures had fallen out and he was trying to find them.[7]

Millions of shares of stock were for sale, but there were few buyers. At times, stock could not be sold at any price.

A total of 16,410,030 shares of stock sold on the New York Stock Exchange that day. "Stock prices virtually collapsed yesterday, swept downward with gigantic losses in the most disastrous trading day in the stock market's history. Billions of dollars in open market values were wiped out as prices crumbled," the front page story in *The New York Times* began.[8] Prices of stocks at other exchanges across the U. S., as well as in Canada and London, also recorded massive losses.

How were billions of dollars lost? Many investors, like Groucho Marx, were forced to sell their stocks at lower prices than they had paid to buy them. Others held on to stocks that had lost value, but they still owned the stocks. Their losses were "paper losses." Alec Wilder, for example, owned stock he had inherited from his father. Before

The trading floor of the New York Stock Exchange as it appeared in 1929. On business days, stock traders bought and sold thousands of shares at the horse-shoe shaped trading posts in the great hall.

the crash, it was worth $160,000. After the crash, Wilder still had his shares, but they were worth much less. Four years later, Wilder's stocks sold for $4,000.[9]

Disappointment and despair overwhelmed investors across the country. Many stories of a wave of suicides followed the crash. Horrible tales circulated of brokers leaping from skyscrapers. After the crash, New York hotel clerks supposedly asked guests if they wanted rooms for jumping or sleeping.[10] Many people may have felt like taking their own lives, but few actually did. When a well-known banker, J. J. Riordan, shot himself, his death was widely publicized. But the suicide rate in October and November in 1929 was actually lower than it was during the previous summer.[11]

The days after October 29 were unsteady for the stock market. Briefly, prices went up, but then they slid again. Stock prices did not reach their lowest point for 1929 until November 13.

It is estimated that in the three weeks in late October and early November 1929, thirty billion dollars in value was lost in U. S. stocks. This means that if you multiplied all the shares of stock by the closing prices on October 19, that total was thirty billion dollars more than it was on November 13.

The loss of thirty billion dollars in value in 1929 was staggering. The entire budget of the U. S. federal government that year was only three billion dollars. The budget was the total amount of money the national government spent for roads, the army, navy, Congress, and all government services.

Depression

"I had no idea my small world would be affected; surely a market crash concerned only the rich," thought Gordon Parks.[1] Parks, a sixteen-year-old African American, was living in St. Paul, Minnesota, in 1929. The son of tenant farmers, Parks had moved to the city after his mother died. He found work at the exclusive Minneapolis Club. In a crisp blue uniform with a striped vest, he served wealthy businessmen who were members there. With this job, Parks could support himself and attend high school.[2]

When Parks arrived at work one October day, a sign was posted in the employees' locker room. "Because of unforeseen circumstances, some personnel will be laid off the first of next month," it read.[3] The notice made the employees uneasy. "By Thursday, the entire world knew. 'MARKET CRASHES — PANIC HITS NATION!' one headline blared," recalled Parks.[4] "Very quickly I, along with millions of others, was without a job. . . . On the seventh of November I went to school and cleaned out my locker. It was impossible to stay on."[5]

As the stock market crashed, the United States was entering the Great Depression. An economic depression is a time when many people are unemployed and business activity declines. The Great Depression was the worst and longest of these economic periods in U. S. history.

The stock market crash did not cause the Great Depression. It was a major event in the same national disaster. The stock market in 1928 and 1929 is often compared to a bubble that got bigger and bigger, and finally popped. When it popped, it

*G*ordon Parks would later become a world famous photographer, writer, and director. This photograph was taken while he worked as a photographer for the United States Farm Security Office.

had several effects. After the crash, people felt a lack of confidence in the economy. They were reluctant to continue buying and spending as they had in the 1920s. This slowdown contributed to businesses producing less and employing fewer people. The crash wiped out the savings of many investors. The collapse of stock prices made it difficult for businesses to raise money. Fewer new businesses started. Many existing ones closed.

A look at the automobile industry reveals how the depression spread. After the crash, people felt like they had less money. They were afraid to pay large sums of money for new cars or take out loans. Automobile sales slowed. Companies slowed down their factories and made fewer cars. They started laying off their workers.

In March 1929, 128,000 workers had jobs at Ford automobile factories in Detroit, Michigan. In December, only 100,000 still had their jobs. Eighteen months later, only 37,000 workers were employed there. From these factories alone, 91,000 people were out of work.[6] Unemployment grew in other industries, too.

Additional problems also plagued the country's economy. Banks were failing. Many families lost their life savings.

Americans were disappointed in the government and especially in President Hoover. Hoover tried to improve the economy. To create new jobs, he increased federal building projects like roads and dams. He tried to get businesses to promise to maintain wages. Hoover's efforts were not enough.

Hoover did not believe that the federal government should give relief to the poor and unemployed. He thought states, cities, and private groups should provide charity. Hoover believed that people should be self-reliant and take care of themselves.

Many tried to be self-supporting. Thousands of unemployed New Yorkers sold apples. They bought crates of apples for $1.75, then sold the fruit for 5 cents apiece. If you sold every apple in your crate, you could make about $1.85 in profits. Six thousand apple sellers worked the streets of New York City.[7]

Wealthy, middle-class, and poor people were all affected by the depression.

"The first thing I noticed about the Depression was that my great-grandfather's house was lost, about to be sold for taxes," said Diana Morgan. Her father was a prosperous cotton merchant in South Carolina. "Our own house was sold. It was considered the most attractive house in town."[8]

Many middle-class people suffered. "I knew the Depression had really hit when the electric lights went out," recalled Robin Langston. "My parents could no longer pay the $1 electric bill."[9] Langston's father owned a restaurant and his mother was a teacher.

When Herbert Hoover was elected president in 1928, many Americans believed that the country would see continued prosperity. Later, Hoover was blamed by many for his ineffectiveness in dealing with the Great Depression.

For the poor, the depression was crushing. Homelessness was rampant. Many families lived in their cars when they lost their houses. "I knew one family there in Oklahoma City," recalled Mary Owsley. "A man and a woman and seven children lived in a hole in the ground."[10] Many homeless traveled the country in empty boxcars on railroad trains. More than 600,000 boys, girls, men, and women rode the rails trying to find work. Thousands of Americans built shacks from old signs, scrap lumber, cardboard, and tin. Communities of these shanties sprouted up around American cities. People called them "Hoovervilles."

During the Great Depression many homeless people built shelters for themselves in temporary communities that became known as Hoovervilles. Approximately one thousand people lived in this Hooverville at the edge of the town dump in Bakersfield, California.

"No one is going hungry," President Hoover claimed. He was wrong. Hunger was one of the worst trials of the Depression. Families scrounged for scraps thrown out by restaurants. Some dug in dumps for food. A schoolteacher told a hungry little girl in the Appalachian Mountains to go home to get food. "I can't," she said, "it's my sister's turn to eat."[11] Millions of Americans ate at soup kitchens run by charities.

President Hoover became very unpopular. People had lost faith in government. Many held Hoover responsible for their suffering. The homeless who slept on park benches covered themselves with discarded newspapers that they called "Hoover blankets." An empty pocket turned inside out, was called a "Hoover flag."[12] Poor Iowa farmers carried signs that said, "In Hoover we trusted, now we are busted."[13]

In 1932, twelve and a half million American workers were unemployed. One of every four families did not have a single wage earner. That year, the stock market reached its lowest point. Each dollar invested in stocks on September 3, 1929, was worth about seventeen cents in July 1932.[14] In November 1932, Herbert Hoover was voted out of the White House.

CHAPTER 6

Today

Today, the brass bell still opens and closes trading on business days at the New York Stock Exchange. Company executives and celebrities usually ring it. They stand on the little balcony where William Crawford stood when the stock market crashed in 1929.

The view from the balcony has changed since Crawford's day. Clusters of computers and monitors have replaced the old horseshoe-shaped trading posts. A digital ticker has replaced the old telegraph. Miles of communication cables carry millions of messages to and from the exchange each day.

The essence of the New York Stock Exchange, though, is unchanged. It is still a bustling marketplace where stocks are bought and sold. Stock sales still require buyers and sellers who agree on price. The New York Stock Exchange and other exchanges have continued to play a vital role in helping companies grow. They have provided the marketplace where the public can share in ownership of those companies.

After 1929, there were changes in the relationship between government and business. Franklin Delano Roosevelt was elected president in 1932. In the following years, Congress passed two new laws regarding stocks. The Securities Act of 1933 required companies selling stock to register and provide certain financial information honestly to the public. The Securities Exchange Act of 1934 created the Securities and Exchange Commission. This commission oversees the U. S. stock markets.

*T*he leadership of President Franklin Delano Roosevelt helped see the United States through the Great Depression.

The Great Depression continued through the 1930s. It finally ended as the U. S. was fighting World War II. Decades passed. The country worked its way through economic ups and downs. Memories of 1929 and the depression lingered. Many wondered if it could happen again.

On Monday, October 19, 1987, they found out. "Wall St. Panic," "CRASH," "Bedlam on Wall St.," read newspaper headlines. "Does 1987 Equal 1929?" asked a front page story in *The New York Times*. In that one day, many stocks lost one-fifth of their value. This was a bigger fall than any single day in 1929. October 19, 1987, was promptly dubbed "Black Monday."

The 1980s had seen significant gains in stock prices. At the same time, there were economic problems in the country. The federal government was spending far more than it was taking in as revenue. Homelessness increased.

Some people involved in the stock market were becoming unbelievably wealthy. Michael Milken, a trader, supposedly made more that $600 million in one year alone. Stories spread that brokers were passing private information and making secret deals. This is called insider trading. It is illegal. Scandals were exposed. Several insiders, including Milken, were arrested.

Stock prices fell fast on October 19, 1987. Some traders described it as "trying to catch a falling knife."[1] Prices began to recover later that year. Fortunately, this crash was not followed by another Great Depression.

In the 1990s, the stock market boomed again. Many large companies grew and merged with other companies The U. S. economy was strong. Growth in the stock market was greater than in the 1920s.[2] Part of this growth was fueled by new technology. Automobiles and electrical appliances changed the country in the 1920s. In the 1990s, personal computers and the Internet changed it.

Home computers had soared in popularity in the 1980s. In the 1990s, they connected to the World Wide

*T*oday, the New York Stock Exchange is the largest stock exchange in the world. Millions of shares of stock are sold there every business day.

Web. New online companies started selling books, plane tickets, and toys. Some new companies were online stock brokerages. With the Internet, people could sit in their homes and buy products like books or clothes, and then go to another Web site and buy stock in the company that sold them those products.

The new online companies became known as dot-coms, because of their Internet addresses. In the 1990s, stocks in many of these companies were offered for sale. Investors leapt at the opportunity. Prices soared. Founders of many of the new companies made fortunes overnight. Many investors expected to make fortunes, too.

Similar to the 1920s, many people in the 1990s stopped looking at factors like profit history when they bought stocks. Like the stock market of the 1920s, the dot-com boom was a bubble.[3] It burst in 2001. Prices fell and paper fortunes disappeared. People who bought high and sold low lost money.

Tragedy struck the country and the stock market later that year. On September 11, 2001, terrorists attacked Washington, D. C., and New York City. Before that day, the Twin Towers of the World Trade Center had stood a few city blocks from the New York Stock Exchange. After 9/11,

*A*fter terrorists attacked the World Trade Center and the Pentagon on September 11, 2001, the New York Stock Exchange displayed this enormous flag over the facade of the building.

the towers were no more. As the country struggled to comprehend what had happened, the exchange closed.

On September 17, New York Governor George Pataki stood on the exchange balcony with World Trade Center rescue workers, Mayor Rudy Giuliani, senators, and other officials.

"Today's ringing of the stock exchange bell sends a powerful message around the globe that America's financial system is far stronger than any cowardly terrorist," said Pataki.[4] Then he rang the opening bell.

Stock prices tumbled after the attacks, but then regained some strength. In 2002, the downturn continued. Concerns about terrorism and the possibility of war contributed to the country's uncertainty. Weak earnings by many companies worried some investors. Still, the decline was seen less as a crash and more as a long bear market. Many investors, though, felt the pain of financial loss.

Even with stock prices down at the end of 2002, the stock market was different from the market in 1929. In 1929, about a million Americans owned stock—roughly one in every hundred people. At the end of 2002, however, an estimated eighty million Americans owned stock. That meant that approximately one in every four Americans, nearly half of all American families, had invested in the nation's businesses. With so many people investing in stocks, it is more important than ever that we understand how the stock market works, and appreciate the effect it has on our everyday lives.

Other Economic Disasters in the United States

DATE	EVENT	DESCRIPTION
1819	Panic	The first major economic crisis in the United States, ending the economic boom that had followed the War of 1812.
1837	Panic	Due in part to irresponsible Western land speculation, 343 of 850 banks in the U. S. fail.
1857	Panic	Several factors contribute to a panic, including the failure of a major insurance and trust company and European speculation in American railroads.
1873	Panic	Jay Cooke & Company, a prominent investment bank, fails. Fifty-seven other stock exchange firms follow. New York Stock Exchange closes for ten days.
1893	Panic	Railroad bankruptcy, withdrawal of European funds from the U. S., and reduction of the country's gold reserves contribute to a panic.
1907	Panic	Several banks and stock brokerages fail. U. S. Treasury and investment bankers cooperate to stabilize conditions. Some bank reform legislation is later passed as a result of the panic.
1987	"Black Monday"	Stock prices plummet on Monday, October 19. The Dow Jones Industrial Average (a leading indicator of stock prices) drops 22.6 percent in one day. (By comparison, the average prices fell 12.9 percent on October 29, 1929.)
2001	Dot-com crash	Prices for many new technology stocks collapse. September 11 terrorist attacks on World Trade Center and Pentagon also contribute to a subsequent drop in stock prices.

Chapter Notes

Chapter 1. Black Thursday

1. Maury Klein, *Rainbow's End* (New York: Oxford University Press, 2001), p. 209.

2. Gordon Thomas and Max Morgan-Witts, *The Day the Bubble Burst* (New York: Doubleday, 1979), p. 357.

3. "Brokerage Houses Are Optimistic," *The New York Times*, October 25, 1929, p. 2.

4. "Weird Roar Surges From Exchange Floor," *The New York Times*, October 25, 1929, p. 3.

5. Gordon Thomas and Max Morgan-Witts, *The Day the Bubble Burst* (New York: Doubleday, 1979), p. 158.

6. Ibid., pp. 366–367.

7. William E. Leuchtenburg, *The Perils of Prosperity, 1914–1932* (Chicago: University of Chicago Press, 1953), p. 245.

Chapter 2. High-Flying Decade

1. Judith S. Baughman, *American Decades 1920–1929* (Detroit: Gale Research, 1996), p. 79.

2. Maury Klein, *Rainbow's End* (New York: Oxford University Press, 2001), p. 116.

3. Ibid., p. 29.

4. William E. Leuchtenburg, *The Perils of Prosperity, 1914–1932* (Chicago: University of Chicago Press, 1953), p. 179.

5. Ibid., p. 187.

6. Klein, p. 83.

7. Frederick Lewis Allen, *Only Yesterday: An Informal History of the Nineteen-Twenties* (New York: Harper & Brothers, 1931), p. 303.

8. Leuchtenburg, p. 178.

9. Ibid., p. 193.

10. Ross M. Robertson, *History of the American Economy* (New York: Harcourt, Brace, Jovanovich, 1955), p. 490.

11. John Kenneth Galbraith, *The Great Crash: 1929* (Boston: Houghton Mifflin, 1954), p. 7.

Chapter 3. "A Sound Money-Making Venture"

1. William K. Klingaman, *1929 The Year of the Great Crash* (New York: Harper & Row, 1989), p. 12.

2. Frederick Lewis Allen, *Only Yesterday: An Informal History of the Nineteen-Twenties* (New York: Harper & Brothers, 1931), pp. 295–297.

3. John Kenneth Galbraith, *The Great Crash: 1929* (Boston: Houghton Mifflin, 1954), p. 22.

4. Klingaman, p. 54.

5. Ibid., p. 67.

6. Allen, p. 315.

7. Charles R. Geisst, *100 Years of Wall Street* (New York: McGraw-Hill, 2000), p. 22.

8. Gordon Thomas and Max Morgan-Witts, *The Day the Bubble Burst* (New York: Doubleday, 1979), p. 274.

Chapter 4. Crash!

1. John Kenneth Galbraith, *The Great Crash: 1929* (Boston: Houghton Mifflin, 1954), pp. 89–90.

2. William K. Klingaman, *1929 The Year of the Great Crash* (New York: Harper & Row, 1989), p. 256.

3. Gordon Thomas and Morgan-Witts, p. 356.

4. Maury Klein, *Rainbow's End* (New York: Oxford University Press, 2001), p. 231.

5. Thomas and Max Morgan-Witts, *The Day the Bubble Burst* (New York: Doubleday, 1979), p. 390.

6. Ibid., pp. 388–89.

7. Ibid., p. 389.

8. "Stocks Collapse in 16,410,030-Share Day," *The New York Times*, October 30, 1929, p. 1.

9. Studs Terkel, *Hard Times: An Oral History of the Great Depression* (New York: Pantheon Books, 1970), p. 198.

10. Galbraith, pp. 131–132.

11. Ibid., p. 134.

Chapter 5. Depression

1. Gordon Parks, *Voices in the Mirror* (New York: Doubleday, 1990), pp. 27–28.

2. Milton Meltzer, *Brother Can You Spare A Dime?* (New York: Alfred A. Knopf, 1969), p. 15.

3. Ibid.

4. Ibid., p. 16.

5. Parks, p. 28.

6. Meltzer, p. 25.

7. T. H. Watkins, *The Great Depression* (Boston: Little Brown & Co., 1993), p. 63.

8. Studs Terkel, *Hard Times: An Oral History of the Great Depression* (New York: Pantheon Books, 1970), p. 172.

9. Ibid., p. 99.

10. Ibid., p. 50.

11. Watkins, p. 57.

12. William E. Leuchtenburg, *The Perils of Prosperity, 1914–1932* (Chicago: University of Chicago Press, 1953), p. 261.

13. Robert Goldston, *The Great Depression: The United States in the Thirties* (Indianapolis: Bobbs Merrill, 1968), p. 86.

14. Gary M. Walton and Roger LeRoy Miller, *Economic Issues in American History* (San Francisco: Canfield Press, 1978), p. 124.

Chapter 6. Today

1. "Is the Party Almost Over?" *Newsweek*, October 26, 1987, p. 50.

2. Charles R. Geisst, *100 Years of Wall Street* (New York: McGraw-Hill, 2000), p. 142.

3. "Dot-com," *Wikipedia: The Free Encyclopedia*, December 14, 2002, <http://wikipedia.org/w/wiki.phtml?title=Dot-com> (January 20, 2003).

4. "Governor Pataki Rings Bell to Open Stock Exchange," *State of New York Banking Department*, September 17, 2001, <http://www.banking.state.ny.us/pr010918.htm> (January 20, 2003).

bear market—When prices paid for stocks are generally going down.

bull market—When prices paid for stocks are generally going up.

economic depression—A time when business activity declines and unemployment increases.

flapper—A modern and unconventional young woman in the 1920s.

installment sale—A credit system for paying debt in multiple payments.

invest—To put money into stocks, real estate, or business, expecting to get an income or profit from it.

investor—A person who invests.

margin—The amount paid by a customer when using a broker's credit to buy a security, such as a share of stock.

overproduction—Producing more goods than are needed or wanted.

panic—Financial crisis when investors rush to turn savings into cash, withdrawing all their savings from banks or selling investments like stocks.

prosperity—A condition of good fortune or wealth.

speculation—Buying something expecting its price to rise.

stock—A piece of ownership in a corporation.

stockbroker—A person who sells stocks for others.

stock exchange—A place where stocks are bought and sold.

stockholder—A person who owns shares of stock in one or more companies.

valet—A personal servant.

Aaseng, Nathan. *The Crash of 1929.* Farmington Hills, Mich.: Gale, 2001.

Blumenthal, Karen. *Six Days in October: The Stock Market Crash of 1929.* New York: Atheneum Books, 2002.

Feinberg, Barbara. *Black Tuesday: The Stock Market Crash of 1929.* Brookfield, Conn.: Millbrook Press, Inc., 1995.

Feinstein, Steven. *The 1930s: From the Great Depression to The Wizard of Oz.* Berkeley Heights, N.J.: Enslow Publishers, Inc., 2001.

Ruth, Amy. *Growing Up in the Great Depression, 1929 to 1941.* Minneapolis, Minn.: The Lerner Publishing Group, 2003.

Woolf, Alex. *The Wall Street Crash, October 29, 1929.* Austin, Tex.: Raintree Steck-Vaughn Publishers, 2002.

Wroble, Lisa A. *The New Deal and the Great Depression in American History.* Berkeley Heights, N.J.: Enslow Publishers, Inc., 2002.

Internet Addresses

The New York Stock Exchange
http://www.nyse.com

The Crash of 1929
http://mypage.direct.ca/r/rsavill/Thecrash.html

The Crash and the Great Depression
http://us.history.wisc.edu/hist102/lectures/lecture18.html

Sliding into the Great Depression
http://econ161.berkeley.edu/TCEH/Slouch_Crash14.html